DreamWorks SHREK

From Screen to Stage

CONTENTS

T0087329

Piano/vocal arrangements by John Nicholas

Cherry Lane Music Company
Director of Publications/Project Editor: Mark Phillips
Project Coordinator: Rebecca Skidmore

ISBN 978-1-60378-285-2

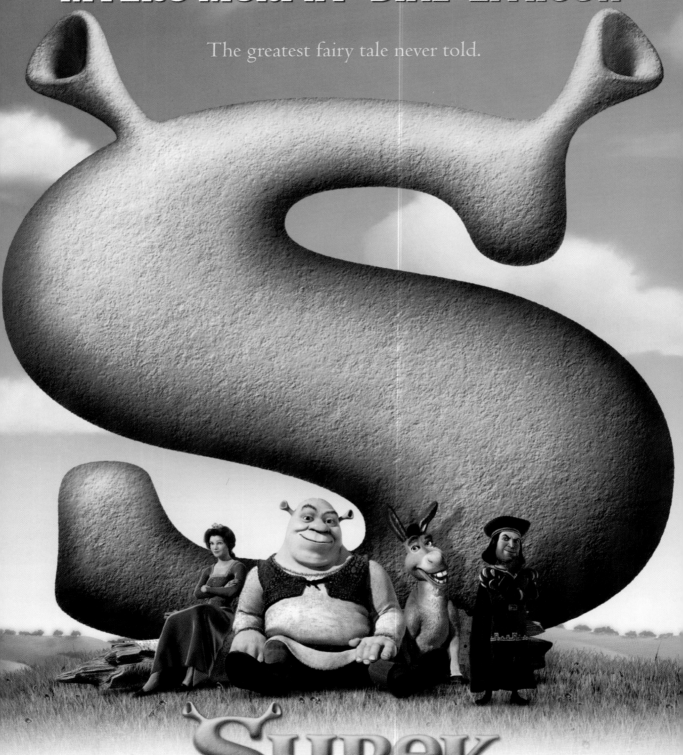

MIKE EDDIE CAMERON JOHN
MYERS MURPHY DIAZ LITHGOW

The greatest fairy tale never told.

SHREK

DREAMWORKS PICTURES PRESENTS A PDI/DREAMWORKS PRODUCTION "SHREK"

ORIGINAL SCORE HARRY GREGSON-WILLIAMS AND JOHN POWELL BASED UPON THE BOOK BY WILLIAM STEIG WRITTEN BY TED ELLIOTT & TERRY ROSSIO
AND JOE STILLMAN AND ROGER S.H. SCHULMAN CO-EXECUTIVE PRODUCER DAVID LIPMAN EXECUTIVE PRODUCERS PENNEY FINKELMAN COX SANDRA RABINS
CO-PRODUCERS TED ELLIOTT TERRY ROSSIO PRODUCED BY ARON WARNER JOHN H. WILLIAMS JEFFREY KATZENBERG DIRECTED BY ANDREW ADAMSON VICKY JENSON

PDI DREAMWORKS   PG PARENTAL GUIDANCE SUGGESTED   DOLBY DIGITAL   WWW.SHREK.COM   SDDS   Soundtrack Available On   DREAMWORKS PICTURES

IT AIN'T OGRE... TIL IT'S OGRE

DREAMWORKS.

SHREK
THE FINAL CHAPTER
3D

In Theatres, reaL D 3D and IMAX 3D

DREAMWORKS ANIMATION SKG PRESENTS A "SHREK FOREVER AFTER" MUSIC BY HARRY GREGSON-WILLIAMS BASED UPON THE BOOK BY WILLIAM STEIG WRITTEN BY JOSH KLAUSNER AND DARREN LEMKE

PG PARENTAL GUIDANCE SUGGESTED
SOME MATERIAL MAY NOT BE SUITABLE FOR CHILDREN
MILD ACTION, SOME RUDE HUMOR AND BRIEF LANGUAGE

EXECUTIVE PRODUCERS ARON WARNER ANDREW ADAMSON JOHN H. WILLIAMS PRODUCED BY GINA SHAY TERESA CHENG DIRECTED BY MIKE MITCHELL

Shrek.com

SOUNDTRACK AVAILABLE ON

DREAMWORKS

MAY 21

Shrek the animated film series is an ogre-sized hit in the film world. Based on the 1990 picture book *Shrek!,* by William Steig, the first film, *Shrek,* won the first-ever Academy Award® for Best Animated Feature. A family favorite for nearly a decade, *Shrek* has so far grossed $266 million domestically and $484 million internationally. Subsequently, each of the next two installments, *Shrek 2* and *Shrek the Third,* topped the opening weekend box office revenue of the original. The series became so popular, in fact, that it inspired the live Broadway production *Shrek the Musical,* which featured Tony-winning actress Sutton Foster as Princess Fiona, Brian d'Arcy James as Shrek, Daniel Breaker as Donkey, and Christopher Sieber as Lord Farquaad, as well as two popular TV specials: "Shrek the Halls" and "Scared Shrekless." The last and final chapter, the animated film *Shrek Forever After,* has already earned more than $238 million, making it the third highest-grossing 3D animated film ever. With its larger-than-life force and momentum, there is seemingly no end in sight for the *Shrek* franchise.

FUN FACTS ABOUT THE FILM SERIES

Shrek

The film consists of 31 sequences and 1,288 shots.

The design of Shrek is similar to that of a bulldog—he has to be ugly and appealing at the same time.

Over 50 sculpts were done of Shrek before they decided on his final look.

Here is a list of all the key fairy-tale/fantasy creatures that appear in the movie:

The Three Bears	Cinderella
Three Blind Mice	Snow White
The Three Little Pigs	The Seven Dwarfs
The Big Bad Wolf	The Pied Piper
Pinocchio	The Gingerbread Man
Gepetto	The Old Woman in the Shoe
Peter Pan	Robin Hood
Tinkerbell	Little John

Over 1,000 fantasy characters invade Shrek's swamp at the beginning of the film.

In addition to the voice of Shrek, Mike Myers also voices one of the Three Blind Mice.

Mike Myers actually read opposite his wife Robin when recording his lines for the climactic love scene at the end of the movie.

Cameron Diaz became very physical when recording her kung fu moves for her scene with Robin Hood and his Merry Men and even broke out into Cantonese at times since she had completed kung fu training during the production of *Charlie's Angels.*

The challenge with John Lithgow was how to figure out how to fit his big, theatrical, dynamic voice into the diminutive, 4 1/2 foot frame of Lord Farquaad. The recording mixers would constantly have to adjust the sound during his recordings to keep track of his booming voice.

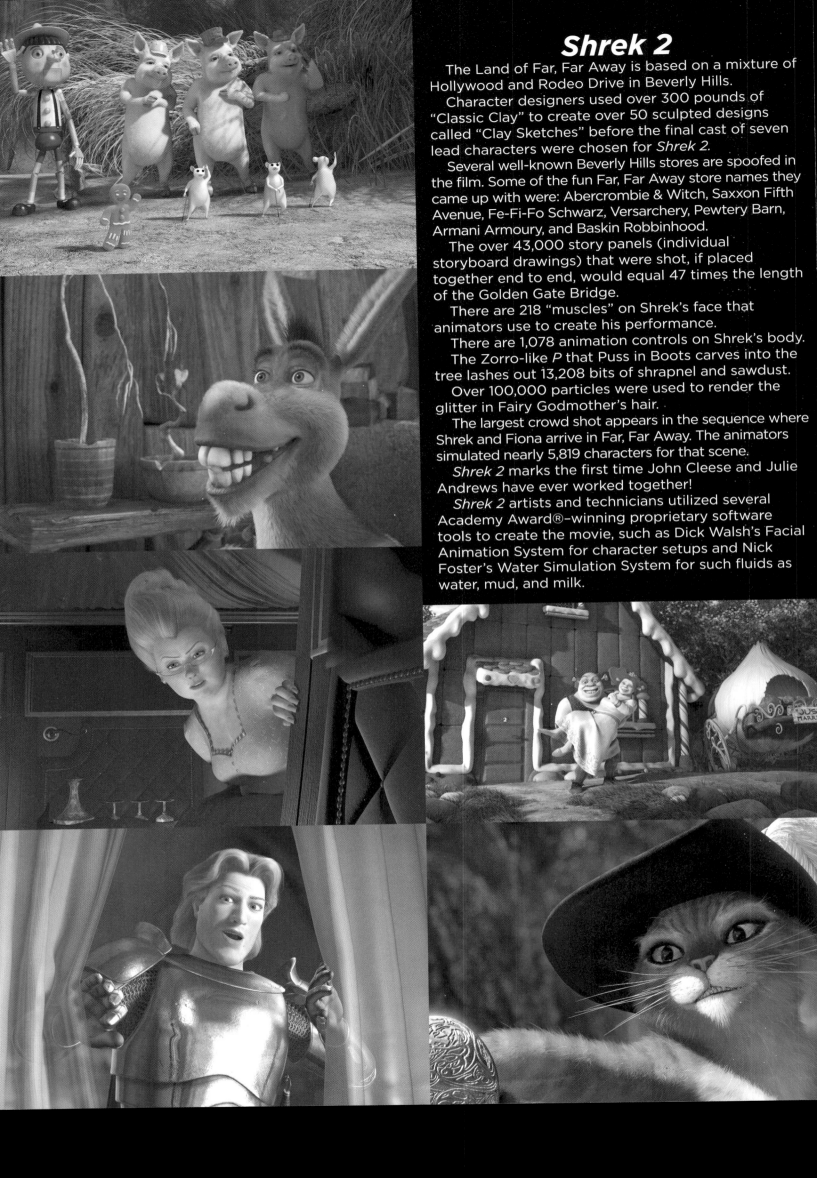

Shrek 2

The Land of Far, Far Away is based on a mixture of Hollywood and Rodeo Drive in Beverly Hills.

Character designers used over 300 pounds of "Classic Clay" to create over 50 sculpted designs called "Clay Sketches" before the final cast of seven lead characters were chosen for *Shrek 2*.

Several well-known Beverly Hills stores are spoofed in the film. Some of the fun Far, Far Away store names they came up with were: Abercrombie & Witch, Saxxon Fifth Avenue, Fe-Fi-Fo Schwarz, Versarchery, Pewtery Barn, Armani Armoury, and Baskin Robbinhood.

The over 43,000 story panels (individual storyboard drawings) that were shot, if placed together end to end, would equal 47 times the length of the Golden Gate Bridge.

There are 218 "muscles" on Shrek's face that animators use to create his performance.

There are 1,078 animation controls on Shrek's body.

The Zorro-like *P* that Puss in Boots carves into the tree lashes out 13,208 bits of shrapnel and sawdust.

Over 100,000 particles were used to render the glitter in Fairy Godmother's hair.

The largest crowd shot appears in the sequence where Shrek and Fiona arrive in Far, Far Away. The animators simulated nearly 5,819 characters for that scene.

Shrek 2 marks the first time John Cleese and Julie Andrews have ever worked together!

Shrek 2 artists and technicians utilized several Academy Award®–winning proprietary software tools to create the movie, such as Dick Walsh's Facial Animation System for character setups and Nick Foster's Water Simulation System for such fluids as water, mud, and milk.

Shrek the Third

The approximate size of the *Shrek the Third* crew was 350.

While some artists got busy animating babies for the film, others got busy, well, having the real thing. A total of 28 babies were born to artists during the making of *Shrek the Third.*

It takes approximately 20,000 man-weeks, or a million man-hours, to animate an entire movie—and this film is no exception!

Over 130,000 frames were created to bring *Shrek the Third* to the big screen.

Shrek and Fiona have been married for eight months by the time *Shrek the Third* starts.

Approximately 4,500 different costumes were originally designed for the crowd scenes in *Shrek the Third,* but only 2,500 made the final "cut."

Twenty-three key fairy-tale/fantasy creatures appear in "Shrek the Third" (with additional dwarves, evil trees, witches, evil knights, and pirates all making appearances throughout the film)! These include:

Puss in Boots	Rapunzel
The Three Little Pigs	Little Red Riding Hood
The Big Bad Wolf	Prince Charming
The Gingerbread Man	Captain Hook
Pinocchio	The Headless Horseman
Three Blind Mice	Rumpelstiltskin
Cinderella	Cyclops
Snow White	Evil Queen
Sleeping Beauty	Ugly Stepsisters

The scene when Dragon and the Dronkeys fly over the theater where Prince Charming is performing features the largest crowd shot in *Shrek the Third,* with 1,373 characters with 2,646 ray-traced eyes and 31,579 individual parts.

There are 4,378 approved men and women in the library of generic characters that animators could chose from to create crowds.

There are 1,602 bricks in the stone docks in the dock sequence.

There are 3,196 bricks in the sewer walls in the sewer sequence when the Princesses escape the castle.

Nine lady cats bid farewell to Puss on the docks.

There are, on average, a total of 62,173 branches and 191,545 leaves per tree.

Shrek the Third takes place in the fall, which reflects the transitional phase in the life of the characters at the heart of the film. (Likewise, the first two films take place in the spring, as the characters' journeys, in many ways, are just beginning.)

Shrek Forever After

There were 65 sequences written, recorded, and storyboarded over the course of the production. The final film has 32.

Nearly 70,000 storyboards were drawn in the making of *Shrek Forever After*.

23 storyboard artists contributed to the film.

Shrek is seven feet tall and has 22 teeth. His hand is about 13.5 inches from the base of his palm to the tip of his middle finger. His shoe size would be a size 22 (15 1/2 inches)—similar to that of Shaquille O'Neal.

Rumpelstiltskin's feet are 6 1/4 inches. That's like a child's size 9 or 10—similar to a 2–3 year old kid.

Rumpelstiltskin wears four different wigs in the movie: business wig, speech wig, angry wig, and victory wig.

Shrek Forever After is the first show that did Cloth, Hair, Finaling, Chains, Smoosh, and Feathers in one show.

Crowd characters have up to three layers of clothing while most hero characters only have one.

The *Shrek Forever After* book was built to have 60 double-sided pages.

There are 241 shields in the ogre ball, with 34 ogres inside it.

In the ogre camp, there are 35 torches in 59 shots. That's 2065 layers, or 4130 for stereo.

DreamWorks Animation software generated 74,016 different ogre variations, of which the same 51 were used throughout all the ogre shots.

There are 430 witches on the dance floor and balconies when Shrek is brought in to meet Rumpelstiltskin.

Reference for the battle between ogres and witches was done with motion capture. Three actors with over 22 years of combined martial arts experience, including one aikido instructor and one U.S. collegiate wushu champion, took part. There were four fully choreographed fights.

Reference for the dancing ogres with Pied Piper was a video of a professional dance troupe with about a dozen members. The choreographer was Michael Rooney, Mickey Rooney's son.

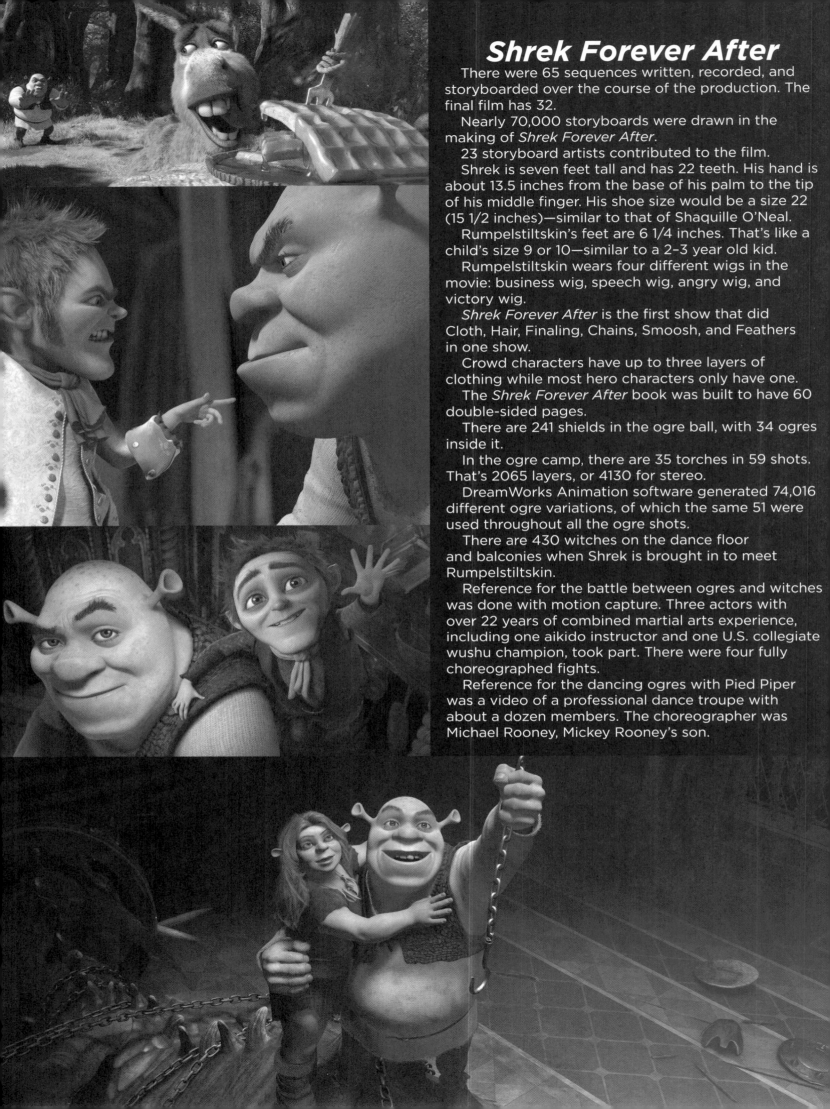

About Shrek The Musical

Shrek The Musical launched its first production on Broadway in December 2008 and has since continued with a U.S. national tour, a planned stay in London's West End beginning in 2011, and other productions throughout the world. The musical takes the Oscar-winning, 80-minute animated film from screen to stage in a full-fledged production with all-new songs, new jokes, and all the beloved characters from the first film for audiences to recognize. Like the film, *Shrek The Musical* also includes material from the 1990 book *Shrek!* by famed New Yorker cartoonist William Steig.

To adapt the characters, story and world of Shrek, DreamWorks turned to composer Jeanine Tesori, of *Thoroughly Modern Millie* and *Caroline or Change* fame, and Pulitzer Prize winner David Lindsay-Abaire, who is behind the clever lyrics and book. They collaborated closely to give a singing voice to Shrek and friends, merging pop influences like R&B and Motown with elements of classic Broadway charm.

Behind the scenes, Tony Award–winning set and costume designer Tim Hatley brought the topnotch animated world of Far, Far Away and Duloc to the stage. In doing so, Hatley faced the challenges of making ogres and witches, princesses and dragons, and a pint-sized villain with a big attitude to life. It takes the actor playing Shrek two hours to get into the ogre make-up and costume. Lord Farquaad performs the entire show on his knees, fitting into a special costume with little legs, and the life-sized Dragon puppet is manned by four actors.

Good conquers evil in this timeless story where being unusual or different is nothing to be ashamed about; and even the ugliest, grumpiest of ogres finds true love and friendship in the most unlikely of circumstances. It celebrates diversity in the vast array of fairy-tale misfits who discover "What makes us special, makes us strong!" and reminds us that "Beautiful ain't always pretty."

I'm a Believer

featured in the DreamWorks Motion Picture SHREK

Words and Music by
Neil Diamond

Moderately slow, with a strong beat

Original key: F# major. This edition has been transposed up one half-step to be more playable.

That's the way it seemed.   Dis - ap - point - ment haunt - ed all ___ my
All you get is pain.   When I want - ed sun - shine, I ___ got

dreams. }   Then I saw her face. ___   Now I'm ___ a be - liev -
rain. }

- er.   Not a trace ___   of doubt ___ in my

mind.   I'm in love.   I'm ___ a be - liev -

13

It Is You
(I Have Loved)
from the DreamWorks Motion Picture SHREK

Words and Music by
Dana Glover, Harry Gregson-Williams,
John Powell and Gavin Greenaway

What an un-ex-pect-ed way on this un-ex-pect-ed day.___ Could it be this is where I____ be-long?

It is you I____ have loved all____ a-long. There's no more mys-ter-y, it is fi-n'lly clear___ to

me. You're the home my heart searched for   so long.

And it is you I have loved   all _____ a - long. _____

_____ There were times   I ran to hide,   a - fraid to

show   the oth - er side,   a - lone in the night _____

All Star

from the DreamWorks Motion Picture SHREK

Words and Music by
Greg Camp

*Recorded a half step lower.

years start com-in' and they don't stop com-in'. Fed to the rules and I hit the ground run-nin'.

Did-n't make sense not to live for fun; your brain gets smart, but your head gets dumb. __

So much to do, so much __ to see, so what's wrong __ with tak - in' the back-streets? You'll

nev - er know if you don't go. You'll nev - er shine if you don't glow.

bod - y once asked could I spare _____ some change for gas, "I need to

get my - self a - way from this place." _____ I said, "Yep, _ what a con-cept! I could use _

_____ a lit - tle fuel my - self and we could all use a lit - tle change." _

_____ Well, the years start com - in' and they don't stop com - in'.

Hallelujah

featured in the DreamWorks Motion Picture SHREK

Words and Music by
Leonard Cohen

1. I've heard there was a se-cret chord ___ that
2.-5. *See additional lyrics*

Da-vid played, ___ and it pleased the Lord, ___ but you don't ___ real-ly

care for mu-sic, ___ do you? ___ It

34

lu - jah. _____ Hal - le - lu - jah. _____

Additional Lyrics

2. Your faith was strong, but you needed proof.
   You saw her bathing on the roof.
   Her beauty and the moonlight overthrew you.
   She tied you to a kitchen chair.
   She broke your throne; she cut your hair.
   And from your lips she drew the Hallelujah. *(To Chorus)*

3. Maybe I have been here before.
   I know this room; I've walked this floor.
   I used to live alone before I knew you.
   I've seen your flag on the marble arch.
   Love is not a victory march.
   It's a cold and it's a broken Hallelujah. *(To Chorus)*

4. There was a time you let me know
   What's real and going on below.
   But now you never show it to me, do you?
   And remember when I moved in you,
   The holy dark was movin' too,
   And every breath we drew was Hallelujah. *(To Chorus)*

5. Maybe there's a God above,
   And all I ever learned from love
   Was how to shoot at someone who outdrew you.
   And it's not a cry you can hear at night.
   It's not somebody who's seen the light.
   It's a cold and it's a broken Hallelujah. *(To Chorus)*

Accidentally in Love

from the Motion Picture SHREK 2

Words and Music by
Adam F. Duritz, Dan Vickrey,
David Immergluck, Matthew Malley
and David Bryson

_____ will fol - low af - ter. Come on, come on, 'cause ev - 'ry - bod - y's af - ter love. _____

So I said _ I'm a snow - ball run - ning, _ run - ning down in - to the spring that's com - ing. All this _ _____ love melt - ing un - der blue skies, belt - ing out sun - light, shim - mer - ing

I'm in love, __ I'm in love, __ I'm in love, __ I'm in love, __ I'm in love, __ I'm in love, __
(I'm in love, __ I'm in love, __ I'm in love.) __

__ ac - ci - den - tal - ly. Come on, come on, spin __ a lit - tle tight - er.

Come on, come on, and the world's __ a lit - tle bright - er. Come on, come on, just get

your - self __ in - side __ her love. __ I'm in love. __

rit. e dim.

42

Holding Out for a Hero

from the Motion Picture SHREK 2

Words by Dean Pitchford

Music by Jim Steinman

Is - n't there a white __ knight up - on a fier - y steed?

Late at night I toss __ and turn __ and dream of what __ I need. _____ I need a

he - ro. I'm hold - ing out for a he - ro till the end of the night. __ He's got-

ta be strong __ and he's got - ta be fast and he's got - ta be fresh __ from the fight. __ I need a

To Coda ⊕

he - ro. I'm hold-ing out for a he - ro till the morn - ing light. ___ He's got-

ta be sure ___ and it's got-ta be soon and he's got-ta be larg - er than life. ___ Larg - er ___ than ___

Doo   doom   da da doom ___ da _____ da doom ka day (yeah).
___   life. ___

Doo   doom   da da doom ___ da _____ da doom ka day.

G5

Some-where af-ter mid-night in my wild-est fan-ta-sy,___

some-where just be-yond___ my reach, there's some-one reach-ing back for me.___

Rac-ing on the thun-der, ris-ing with the heat,___

D.S. al Coda

it's gon-na take a su-per-man___ to sweep me off___ my feet._____ I need a

Coda

life.

G5

(Spoken:) Up where the moun-tains meet the heav-ens a-bove, out where the light-ning ___ splits the sea,

I would swear that there's some-one some-where watch-ing me. ___

Through the wind and the chill and the ___ rain and the storm and the ___ flood,

47

I can feel his ap-proach like fi - re in my blood.

Doo doom da da doom da da doom ka day (yeah).

da doom ka day. I need a he - ro. I'm hold-ing out for a he-

ro till the end of the night. He's got - ta be strong and he's got - ta be fast and he's

got - ta be fresh _ from the fight. _ I need a he - ro. I'm hold-ing out for a he -

ro till the morn - ing light. _ He's got - ta be sure _ and it's got - ta be soon and he's

1. got - ta be larg - er than life. _ I need a 2. got - ta be larg - er than life. _

Larg - er _ than _

_ life. _

Fairy Godmother Song

from the Motion Picture SHREK 2

Words and Music by Andrew Adamson,
Harry Gregson-Williams, Stephen Barton,
Dave Smith, Walt Dohrn and Aron Warner

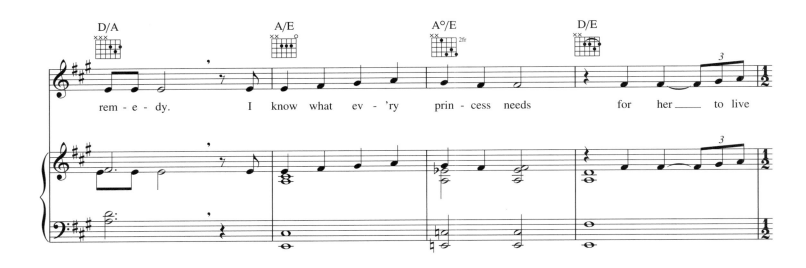

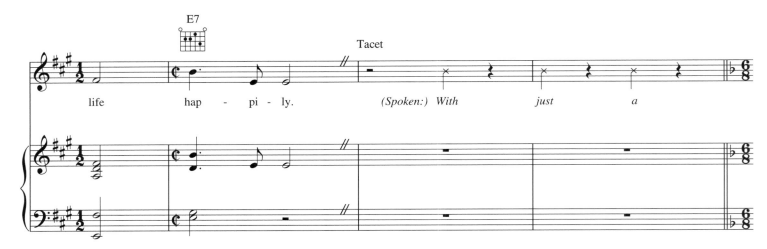

bath - room wall.
(Spoken:) For a happy ever after, give Fiona a call!

A sport - y car - riage to ride in style, a sex - y man boy chauf - feur ___ "Kyle." We'll ban - ish your blem - ish - es, tooth de - cay. Cel - lu - lite thighs will fade a - way, and oh what the hey... Have a Bi - chon Fri -

cresc.

f

sé! Nip and tuck here and there, to

land that prince with the per - fect hair. Lip - stick lin - ers, shad - ows, blush, to

get that prince with the sex - y tush. Luck - y day, hunk buf - fet.

You and your prince take a roll in the hay. You can spoon on the moon

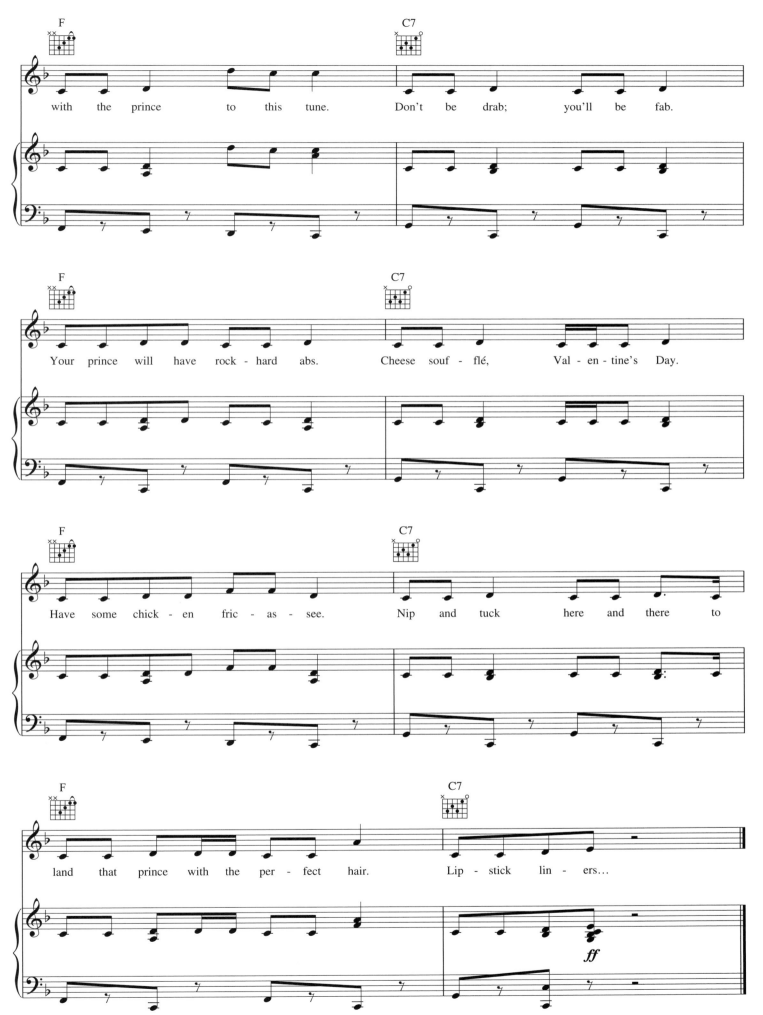

Livin' la Vida Loca

from the Motion Picture SHREK 2

Words and Music by
Desmond Child and Robi Rosa

prem - o - ni - tion.   That girl's gon - na make me fall. __
new ad - dic - tion   for ev - 'ry

day and night. __ She'll

make you take __ your clothes __ off   and go danc - ing in the rain. __

She'll make you live __ her cra - zy life, __ but she'll

take a - way your pain ____ like a bul - let ____ to ____ your brain. ____

Up - side, ____ in - side out, she's

liv - in' la vi - da lo - ca. She'll push and ____ pull ____

____ you down, liv - in' la vi - da lo - ca. Her

New York Cit - y   in a funk - y cheap mo - tel. ___

make you go ___ in - sane. ___ Up - side, ___ in - side out, she's

liv - in' la vi - da lo - ca. She'll push and ___ pull ___

___ you down, liv - in' la vi - da lo - ca. Her lips are ___ dev -

il red and her skin's the col - or of mo - cha. And she will ___ wear ___

62

Royal Pain

from the Motion Picture SHREK THE THIRD

Words and Music by
Mark Everett

I got some sleep and I need-ed it. ___ Not a lot, just a

lit - tle bit. Some-one's al - ways try - in' to keep me from it. It's a cry-

the on-ly thing I was born to do. And they're all in - sane. Such a roy - al pain in the neck. I'm just try-in' to get by with my pride a lit-tle bit in-tact.

Barracuda

from the Motion Picture SHREK THE THIRD

Words and Music by
Nancy Wilson, Ann Wilson,
Michael Derosier and Roger Fisher

kiss-es for real. _____ And tales, _____ it nev-er
sell-ing a song, _____ a name. Whis-per

fails! You ly-ing so low in __ the weeds._
game. And if the real thing don't do the trick,_

_____ I bet you gon-na am-bush_ me. _____ You'd have me
you bet-ter make up some-thing_ quick. _____ You gon-na

down, down,_ down, ___ down on my __ knees. Now would-n't you,
burn, burn,_ burn,___ burn it to the wick. Ooh,

Tacet   *To Coda* ⊕

Bar-ra-
Bar-ra-

I think that you got the blues _____ too. _

All that _ night _ and all the next, swam with-out look-ing back.

Made for the west-ern pools.

Sil - ly, sil - ly fools. _

D.S. 𝄋 *(lyric 2) al Coda* 𝄌

Coda

The

cu - da.

Live and Let Die

from the Motion Picture SHREK THE THIRD

Words and Music by
Paul McCartney and Linda McCartney

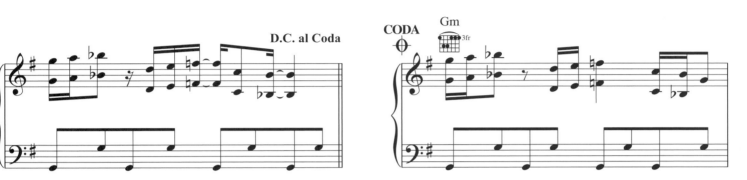

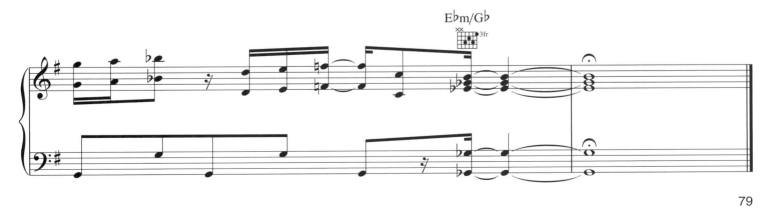

Cat's in the Cradle

from the Motion Picture SHREK THE THIRD

Words and Music by
Harry Chapin and Sandy Chapin

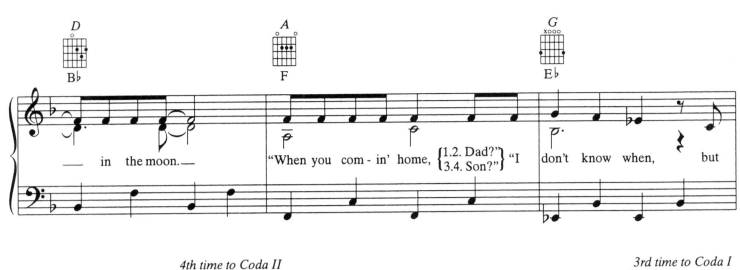

in the moon. "When you com-in' home, {1.2. Dad?"} "I don't know when, but
3.4. Son?"}

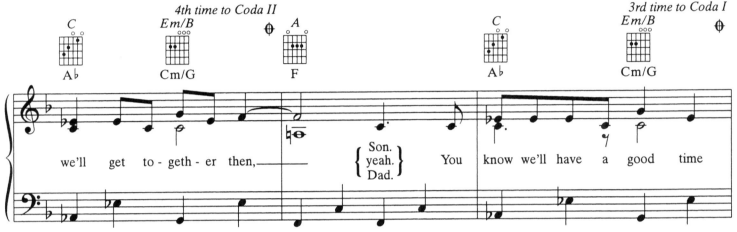

4th time to Coda II   3rd time to Coda I

we'll get to-geth-er then,_____ {Son. yeah. Dad.} You know we'll have a good time

then."

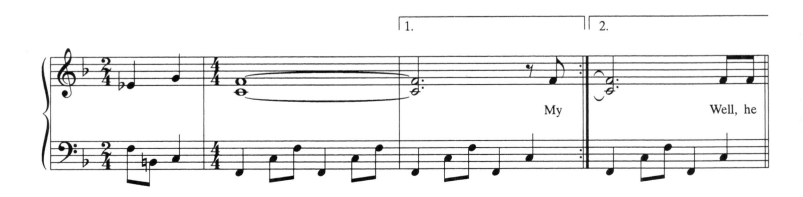

1.   2.

My   Well, he

D.S. al Coda I

Coda

then."

Slower

I've long since re-tired, my son's moved a-way.

I called him up just the oth-er day.

I said, "I'd like to see___ you if

you don't mind." He said, "I'd love to, Dad, if I can find the time.

You see, my new job's a has-sle and the kids have the flu, but it's

sure nice talk-in' to you, Dad. It's been sure nice talk-in' to

you." And as I hung up the phone it oc-

mp

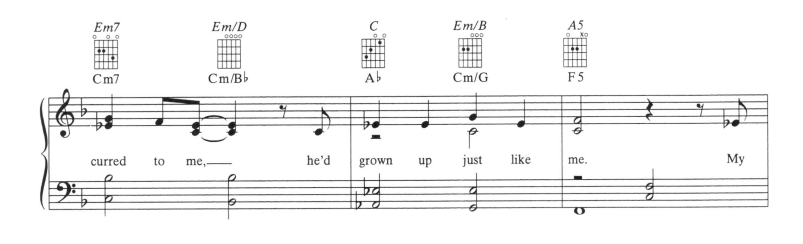

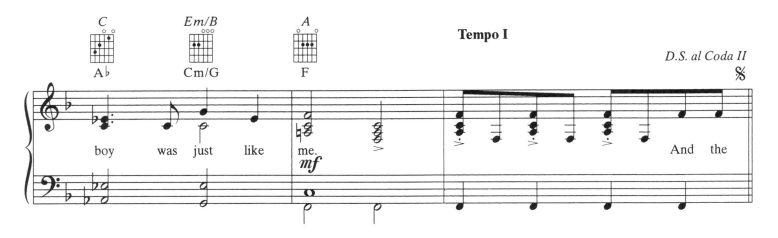

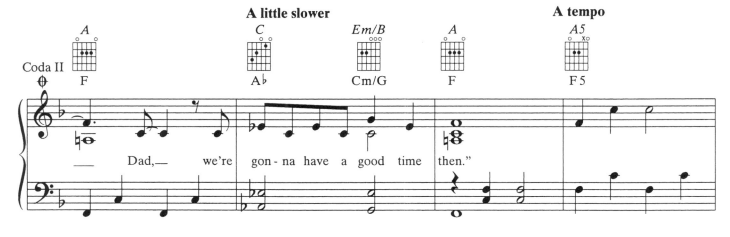

Isn't It Strange

from SHREK FOREVER AFTER

Words and Music by
Scott D. Hoffman and Jason Sellards

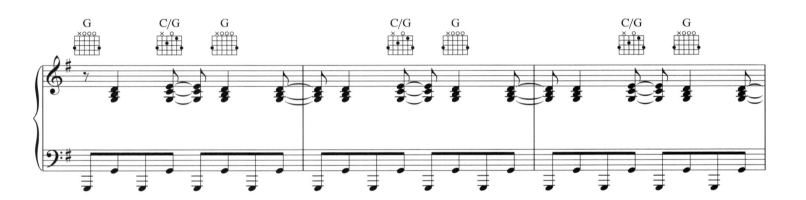

love it when it laughs ___ and it says ___ my name. ___ Well, if you
just dis - ap - peared, ___ I'd have to cry a mil - lion tears. ___ At least
day out - side ___ with - out my face in the grass. ___ And you can

say it a - gain, ___ well, it's just ___ my thing, ___ and so do ___
one would fall, ___ like a great ___ big toll; ___ they can love ___
bet me, babe, ___ when the leaves fall down, ___ you can

___ the tel - e - gram; ___ it danc - es and sings, ___ sing - in',
___ them - selves, ___ grow - ing big ___ e - nough to grow; scream - in',
pick my food; ___ for you ap - ples, figs, and ber - ries, sing - in',

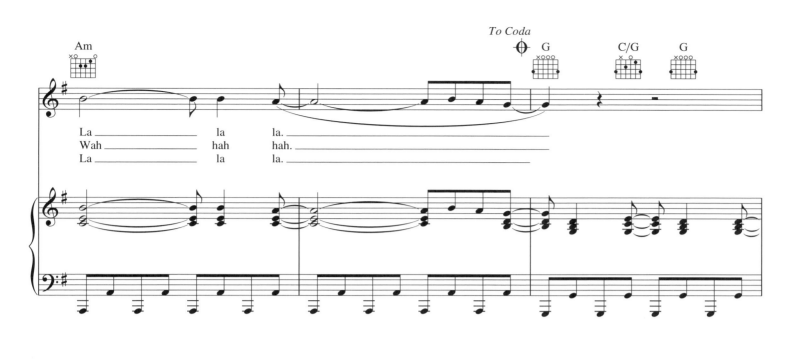

La _____ la la. _____
Wah _____ hah hah. _____
La _____ la la. _____

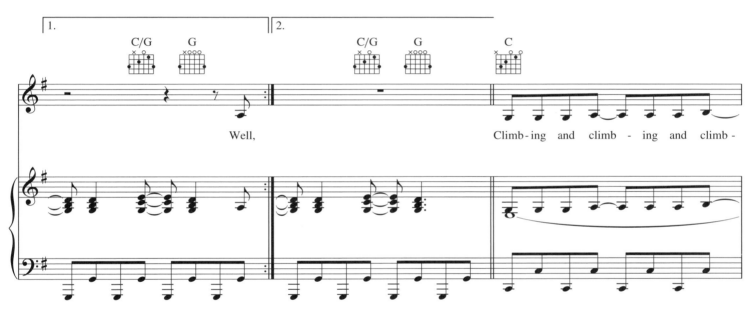

Well,

Climb - ing and climb - ing and climb -

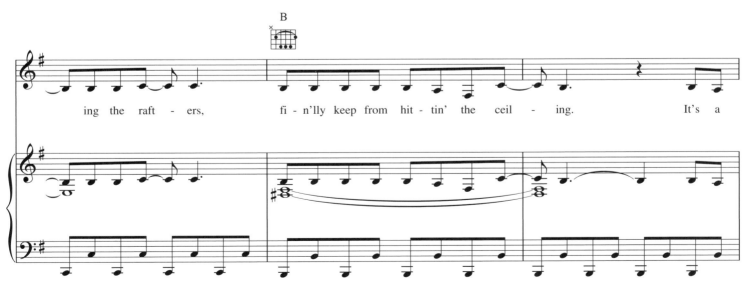

ing the raft - ers, fi - n'lly keep from hit - tin' the ceil - ing. It's a

Darling I Do

from SHREK FOREVER AFTER

Music by
Landon Pigg and Lucy Schwartz

Shapes in the sky ____ looked plain to my ____ eyes. ____ The world had less col - or with - out ____ you.

I know plen - ty of peo - ple with eyes closed. They don't see you like I ____

Play 1st time only

D.S. al Coda II

I   know   plen - ty   of   peo   -   ple   with   eyes __

__ closed.   They   don't   see   you   like - a...

Right Back Where We Started From

from SHREK FOREVER AFTER

Words and Music by
Vince Edwards and Pierre Tubbs

101

I Know It's Today

from SHREK THE MUSICAL

Words by
David Lindsay-Abaire

Music by
Jeanine Tesori

Moderately fast

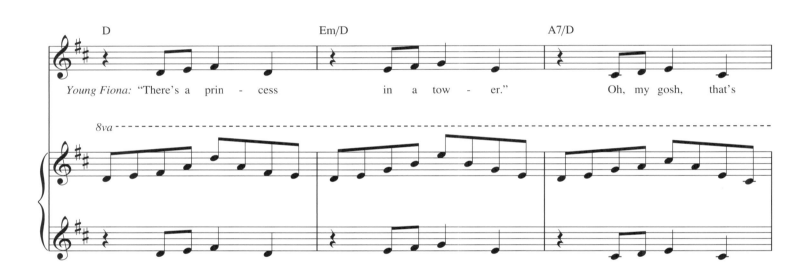

Young Fiona: "There's a prin - cess in a tow - er." Oh, my gosh, that's

just like me. "Poor Ra - pun - zel needs a hair - cut,

by can - dle - light. ___ My white ___ knight and his steed ___

will look just like ___ these pic - tures. ___ It

won't be _____ long ___ now, I guar - an - tee. _____

Day num - ber twen - ty - three. ___

I know it's to - day, ___

I know it's to -

day. ___

Teen Fiona: "There's a prin - cess in a co - ma." Glad it's her in -

prince is good at kiss - ing and melt - ing Snow White's

heart. So I know ___ he'll ap - pear ___ and his

ar - mor will ___ be blind - ing, ___ as shin - ing as ___

___ his per - fect teeth ___ and man - ly hose. ___ He'll pro - pose ___

He'll show up to - day. ____

Adult Fiona: Ay. ____ There's a prin - cess,

an - y prin - cess, take your pick, they're all like me.

Not ex - act - ly. I'm still wait - ing; they're out liv - ing

I be - lieve the sto - ry - books I read _____ by can - dle - light. _____

_____ My white ___ knight, my knight and his steed _____ will

look just like ___ these pic - tures. ___ It won't be _____ long ___

now, I guar - an - tee. _____ *Young Fiona:* Day num - ber

116

day, _____ ooh. _____ I know it's _____ to -

_____ I know it's _____ to - day, _____ ooh. _____

ooh. _____ I know it's _____ to - day. _____

day. I know it's _____ to - day. _____

_____ I know it's _____ to - day.

I know it's _____ to - day.

Who I'd Be

from SHREK THE MUSICAL

Words by
David Lindsay-Abaire

Music by
Jeanine Tesori

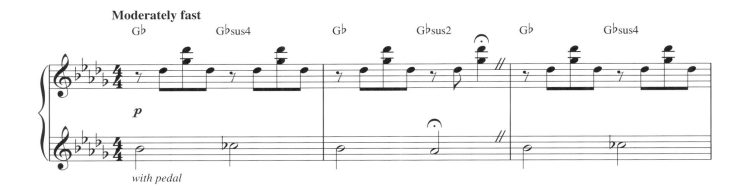

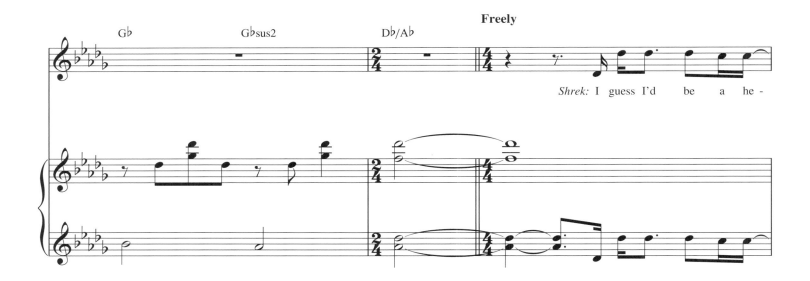

dash-ing,   a shield with-in ___ my grip. ___   Or else, I'd   be a Vi-

king   and live a life ___ of   der - ring,   while smell-ing like a

Moderately, in tempo

her - ring.   Up-on a Vi - king   ship I'd sail a-way.   I'd see the world.

I'd reach the far - thest reach - es.   I'd feel the wind,   I'd taste the

salt and sea _____ and may - be storm _____ some

beach - es. That's who I'd be. That's who I'd

be. Or I could be _____ a po - et and write a dif - f'rent

sto - ry, one that tells _____ of glo - ry and wipes a - way _____ the lies. _____

it all _____ while rhym - ing. But we all

learn. But we all learn.

An o - gre al - ways hides. An o - gre's fate ___ is known.

An o - gre al - ways stays in the dark and all ___ a -

lone.

So yes, I'd be a he - ro. And if my wish were grant-

ed, life would be ___ en - chant - ed, or so the sto - ries say. ___

Of course, I'd be a he - ro, and I would scale ___ a

124

love. We'd feel the stars __ as- cend - ing. We'd share a kiss, I'd find my

des - ti - ny. _____ I'd have _____ a he - ro's end -

ing, _____ a per - fect hap - py

end - ing. That's how it would be, a

big bright beau - ti - ful world. _____

But not for me. _____

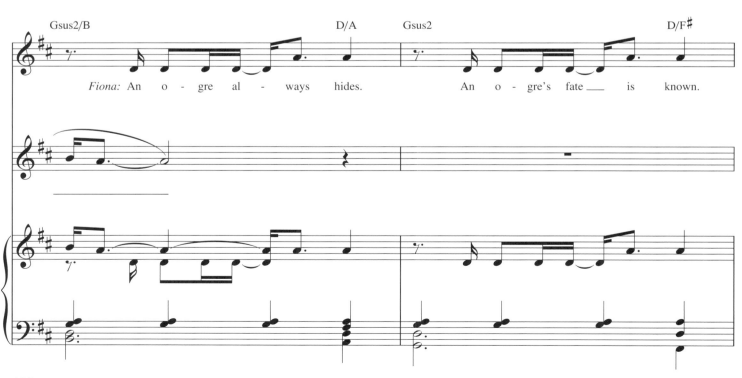

Fiona: An o - gre al - ways hides. An o - gre's fate ___ is known.

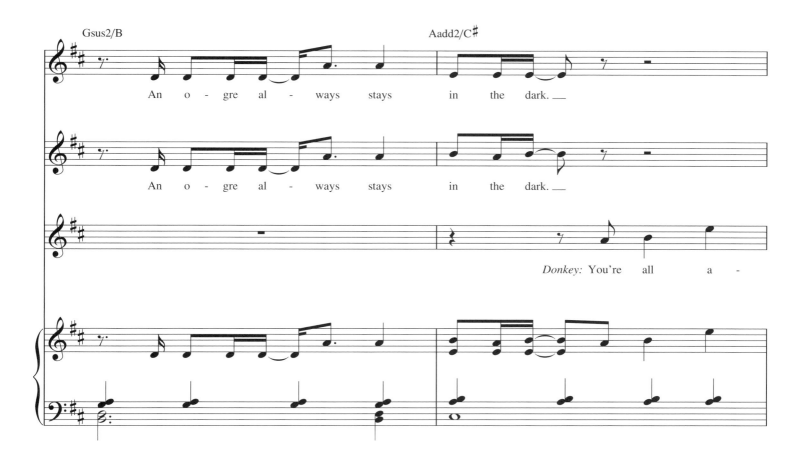

An o - gre al - ways stays in the dark. ___

An o - gre al - ways stays in the dark. ___

Donkey: You're all a -

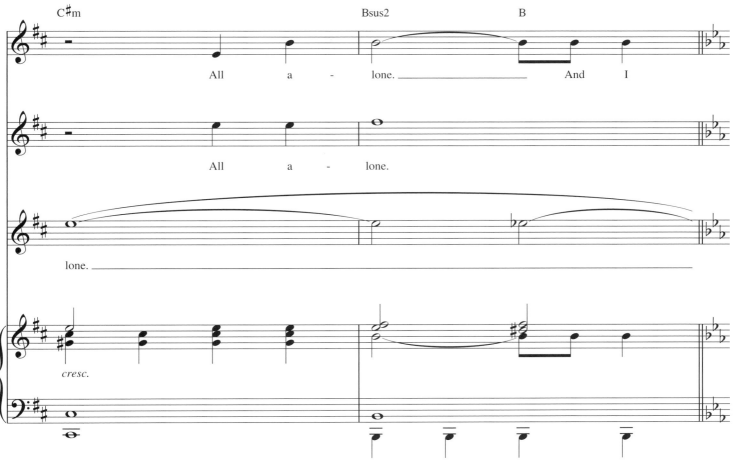

All a - lone. ___ And I

All a - lone.

lone. ___

cresc.

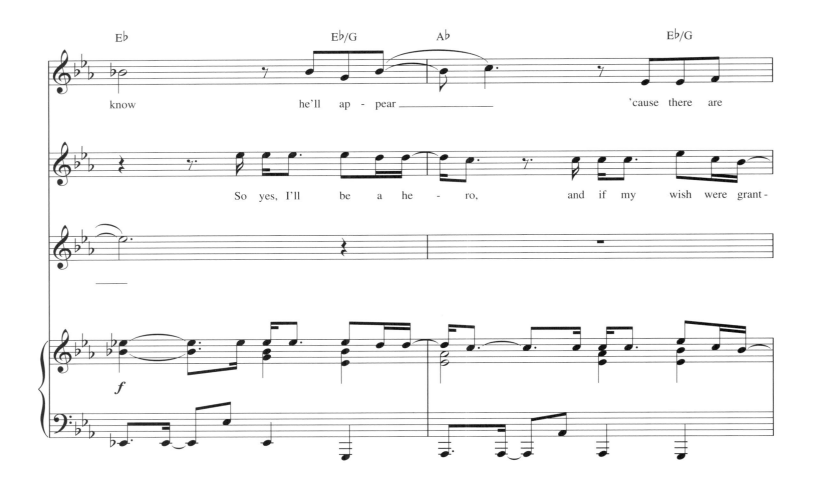

I be-lieve the sto - ry-books I

Of course, I'd be a he - ro, and I would scale _ a

You need a pal, my cal - en - dar's o - pen. _____

read by can - dle - light. _____

tow - er to save a hot - house flow - er and car - ry her __ a - way. __

Ya need

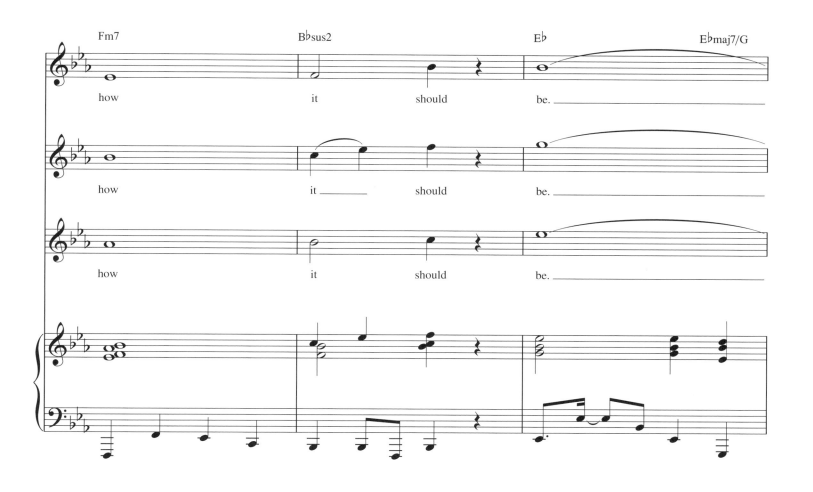

how   it   should   be. _____

how   it _____   should   be. _____

how   it   should   be. _____

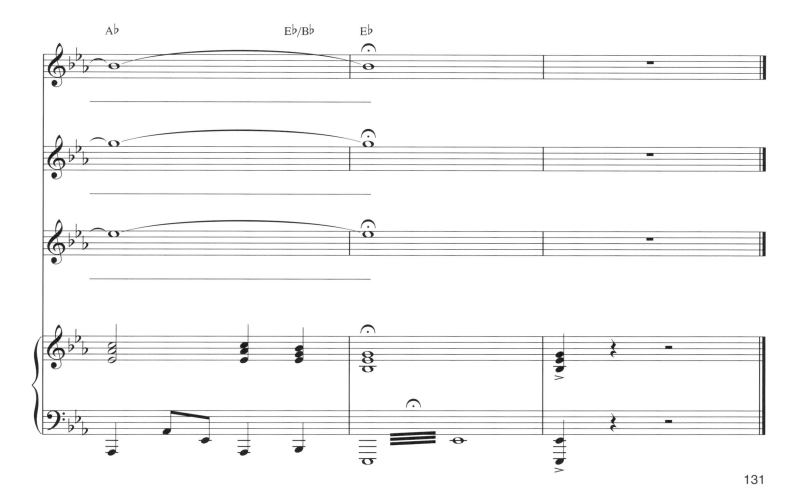

Freak Flag

from SHREK THE MUSICAL

Words by
David Lindsay-Abaire

Music by
Jeanine Tesori

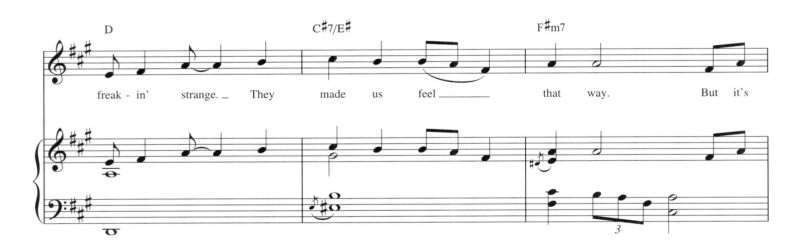

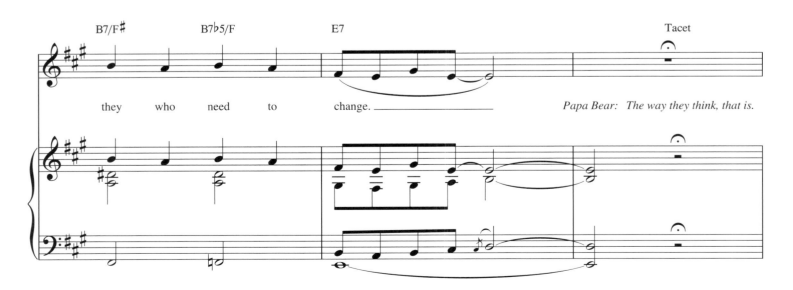

135

er take it down, nev-er take it down. Raise it way _____ up high. _____

_____ Let your freak _ flag fly. _____

3 Pigs: I'm proud to be a pig - gy. Lit-tle pig, lit-tle

Papa Bear: pig. I raise my _____ fur-ry fist. _____ *All:* Pa-pa Bear, Pa-pa

freak flag wave. ___ Let your freak flag fly. ___

Nev - er take it down, nev - er take it down. Raise it way ___

Moderately slow, in 2
(♩ = ♩.)

___ up high. ___

Pinocchio: Yes, it

Ooh, ooh. ___

___ all makes sense now. We may be freaks,

but we're freaks with teeth

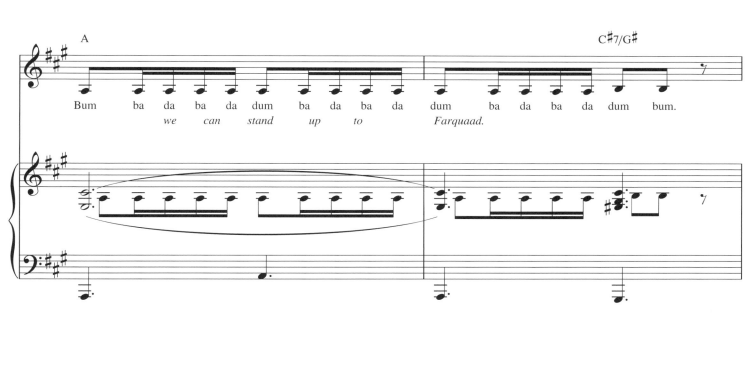

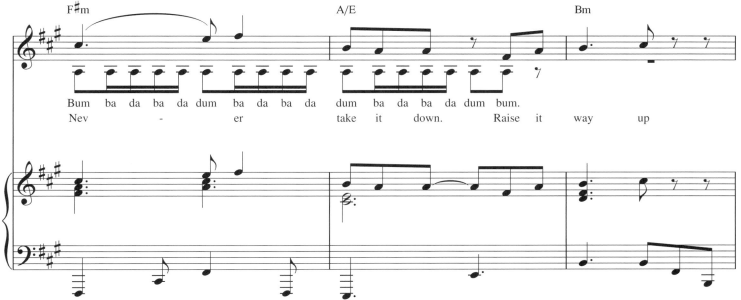

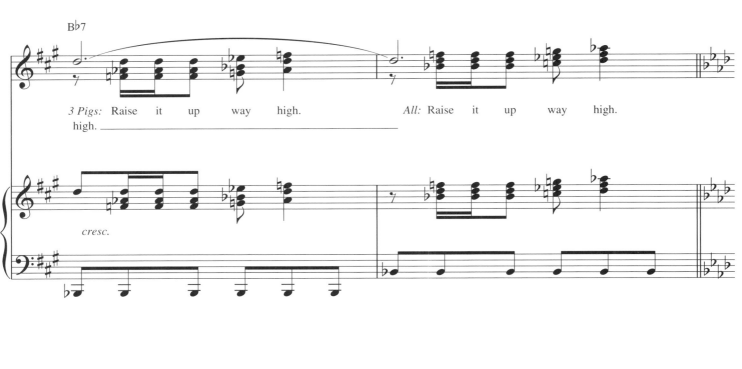

3 Pigs: Raise it up way high. *All:* Raise it up way high.
high.

Humpty Dumpty: We've got mag - ic. We've got pow - er Who are they _____ to
All: (Ooh. _____

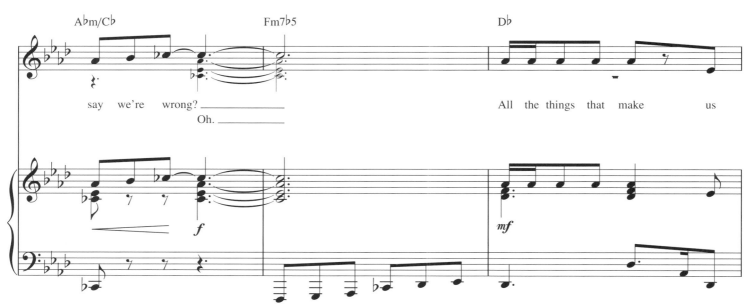

say we're wrong? _____ All the things that make   us
Oh. _____

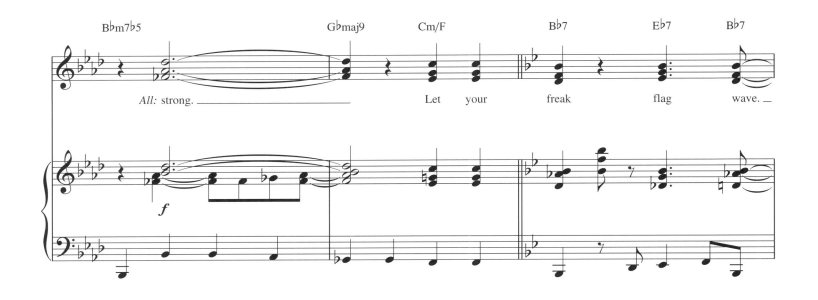

All: strong. _____ Let your freak flag wave. _

_ Let your freak flag fly. _____ Nev -
Nev -

er take it down, nev - er take it down. Raise it way _____ up high. _
er take it down. _____

More Great Piano/Vocal Books

FROM CHERRY LANE

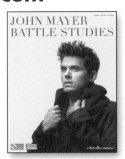

For a complete listing of Cherry Lane titles available, including contents listings, please visit our web site at
www.cherrylane.com

See your local music dealer or contact:

7777 W. BLUEMOUND RD. P.O. BOX 13819 MILWAUKEE, WI 53213

Prices, contents and availability subject to change without notice.

1210